Wisdom

summersdale

WISDOM

Summersdale Publishers Ltd
46 West Street
Chichester
West Sussex
PO19 1RP
UK

www.summersdale.com

Printed and bound in China

ISBN: 978-1-84953-033-0

Substantial discounts on bulk quantities of Summersdale books are available to corporations, professional associations and other organisations. For details contact Summersdale Publishers by telephone: +44 (0) 1243771107, fax: +44 (0) 1243 786300 or email: nicky@summersdale.com.

Wisdom

thoughts & quotations
for every day

*Make each day both useful and pleasant,
and prove that you understand the worth of
time by employing it well.*

Louisa May Alcott

Knowledge comes but wisdom lingers.

Alfred Tennyson

It takes courage to face one's own shortcomings, and wisdom to do something about them.

Edgar Cayce

We are made wise not by the recollection of our past, but by the responsibility for our future.

George Bernard Shaw

We can do no great things, only small things with great love.

Mother Teresa

The highest form of wisdom is kindness.

The Talmud

There are three ingredients in the good life:
learning, earning and yearning.

Christopher Morley

We carry within us the wonders we seek without us.

Sir Thomas Browne

The only gift is a portion of thyself.

Ralph Waldo Emerson

*You must be the change you want to see
in the world.*

Mahatma Gandhi

The greater the obstacle, the more glory in overcoming it.

Molière

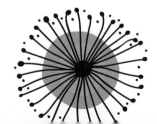

Our lives begin to end the day we become silent about things that matter.

Martin Luther King Jr

Wise men learn many things from their enemies.

Aristophanes

The more we see, the more we are capable of seeing.

Maria Mitchell

True religion is real living; living with all one's soul, with all one's goodness and righteousness.

Albert Einstein

The most decisive actions of our life... are most often unconsidered actions.

André Gide

Be happy. It's one way of being wise.

Colette

Science is organised knowledge. Wisdom is organised life.

Immanuel Kant

If your compassion does not include yourself, it is incomplete.

Buddha

You cannot find peace by avoiding life.

Virginia Woolf

It is not because things are difficult that we do not dare; it is because we do not dare that they are difficult.

Seneca

To be what we are, and to become what we are capable of becoming, is the only end of life.

Robert Louis Stevenson

We learn wisdom from failure much more than success.

Samuel Smiles

By attempting the impossible one can attain the highest level of the possible.

August Strindberg

Turn your ear to wisdom and apply your heart to understanding.

Proverbs 2:2

The highest result of education is tolerance.

Helen Keller

The good life is one inspired by love and guided by knowledge.

Bertrand Russell

Kindness is more important than wisdom, and the recognition of this is the beginning of wisdom.

Theodore Rubin

*Only a life lived
for others is a life
worthwhile.*

Albert Einstein

We make a living by what we get, but we make a life by what we give.

Winston Churchill

It is strange how often a heart must be broken before the years can make it wise.

Sara Teasdale

*Knowledge is a process of piling up facts;
wisdom lies in their simplification.*

Martin Fischer

It's more important to do the right thing than to do things right.

Peter Drucker

Wonder is the beginning of wisdom.

Socrates

Better than a hundred years of idleness
Is one day spent in determination.

The Dhammapada

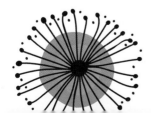

Dare to be wise: when you begin you are already halfway there.

Horace

Beauty endures only for as long as it can be seen; goodness, beautiful today, will remain so tomorrow.

Sappho

A man's true wealth… is the good that he does in this world to his fellows.

Muhammad

*Great works are performed not by strength
but by perseverance.*

Samuel Johnson

Speak few words, but say them with quietude and sincerity and they will be long-lasting.

Lao Tzu

*Vanity is the quicksand
of reason.*

George Sand

*Life is so constructed that an event does
not, cannot, will not, match
the expectation.*

Charlotte Brontë

All human wisdom is summed up in two words — wait and hope.

Alexandre Dumas, *Père*

Nothing happens unless first we dream.

Carl Sandburg

Life is like playing a violin solo in public,
and learning the instrument as
one goes on.

Samuel Butler

Patience is the
companion of wisdom.

St Augustine of Hippo

If you do not tell the truth about yourself you cannot tell it about other people.

Virginia Woolf

What is the meaning of life? To be happy and useful.

Dalai Lama

*It is cowardice to
perceive what is right
but not to do it.*

Confucius

Honour has not to be won: it must only not be lost.

Arthur Schopenhauer

*Courage without
conscience is a
wild beast.*

Robert G. Ingersoll

People grow through experience if they meet life honestly and courageously. This is how character is built.

Eleanor Roosevelt

No act of kindness, no matter how small,
is ever wasted.

Aesop

Reject your sense of injury and the injury itself disappears.

Marcus Aurelius

*One must be poor to know the luxury
of giving.*

George Eliot

When you are good to others you are best to yourself.

Benjamin Franklin

He who masters others has power. He who masters himself has strength.

Lao Tzu

Life begets life. Energy creates energy. It is by spending oneself that one becomes rich.

Sarah Bernhardt

As soon as you trust yourself, you will know how to live.

Johann Wolfgang von Goethe

You cannot run away from weakness; you must some time fight it out or perish.

Robert Louis Stevenson

Do not learn how to react, but how to respond.

Buddha

If you have knowledge, let others light their candles in it.

Margaret Fuller

Power without wisdom collapses under its own weight.

Horace

*The greatest mistake you can make in life
is to be continually fearing you will
make one.*

Elbert Hubbard

Never apologise for showing feeling. When you do so, you apologise for the truth.

Benjamin Disraeli

The truest greatness lies in being kind, the truest wisdom in a happy mind.

Ella Wheeler Wilcox

A wise man turns chance into good fortune.

Thomas Fuller

Pleasure in the task puts perfection in the work.

Aristotle

Memory is the mother of all wisdom.

Aeschylus

The only certainty is that nothing is certain.

Pliny the Elder

He who knows others is learned; he who knows himself is wise.

Lao Tzu

Life was meant to be lived and curiosity must be kept alive. One must never, for whatever reason, turn his back on life.

Eleanor Roosevelt

The real voyage of discovery consists not in seeking new landscapes but in having new eyes.

Marcel Proust

Wisdom is oftentimes nearer when we stoop than when we soar.

William Wordsworth

There is nothing that will not reveal its secrets if you love it enough.

George Washington Carver

*Forgiveness is a virtue
of the brave.*

Indira Gandhi

The surest test of discipline is its absence.

Clara Barton

Honesty is the first chapter in the book of wisdom.

Thomas Jefferson

There is not a heart but has its moments of longing, yearning for something better, nobler, holier than it knows now.

Henry Ward Beecher

The strongest principle of growth lies in human choice.

George Eliot

To conquer fear is the beginning of wisdom.

Bertrand Russell

To enjoy freedom… we have to control ourselves.

Virginia Woolf

A wise man makes his own decisions, an ignorant man follows the public opinion.

Chinese proverb

And in the end, it's not the years in your life that count. It's the life in your years.

Abraham Lincoln

All men by nature desire knowledge.

Aristotle

Without courage, wisdom bears no fruit.

Baltasar Gracián

Be faithful in small things because it is in them that your strength lies.

Mother Teresa

Wise men talk because they have something to say; fools, because they have to say something.

Plato

Do what you can, with what you have, where you are.

Theodore Roosevelt

*Listen or your tongue
will keep you deaf.*

Native American proverb

I think one's feelings waste themselves in words; they ought all to be distilled into actions and into actions which bring results.

Florence Nightingale

Be not afraid of life.
Believe that life is worth
living, and your belief
will help create the fact.

Henry James

Have you enjoyed this book? If so, why not write a review
on your favourite website?

Thanks very much for buying this
Summersdale book.

www.summersdale.com